English as a Second F*cking Language

English as a Second F*cking Language

by Sterling Johnson
(and a distinguished panel of experts)

St. Martin's Griffin ⚏ New York

A THOMAS DUNNE BOOK.
An imprint of St. Martin's Press.

ENGLISH AS A SECOND F*CKING LANGUAGE.
Copyright © 1995 by Sterling Johnson. All rights
reserved. Printed in the United States of America.
No part of this book may be used or reproduced in
any manner whatsoever without written permission
except in the case of brief quotations embodied in
critical articles or reviews. For information,
address St. Martin's Press, 175 Fifth Avenue,
New York, N.Y. 10010.

Library of Congress
Cataloging-in-Publication Data

Johnson, Sterling.
English as a second f*cking language / by
Sterling Johnson.
p.   cm.
ISBN 0-312-14329-X
1. Swearing.   2. English language—
Obscene words.   I. Title.
[PE3724.S85J65   1996]
427'.09—dc20   96-7126
                                          CIP

First published in the United States of America by
ESFL University Press

10   9

English as a Second F*cking Language

Introduction

Those who learn English as a second language from traditional textbooks are often at a loss when they hear a conversation such as the following:

Night at the Opera*

John: Mary, would you like to attend the opera this evening?

Mary: Fucking-A. Should I wear my black dress?

John: Why the fuck not?

Mary: Fucked if I know—Oh, fuck! I just remembered. It got fucked up in the wash.

John: Well, fuck the opera, let's stay home and fuck.

Mary: Good fucking idea.

---

* A fuck-by-fuck analysis of **Night at the Opera** will be found at the end of the FUCK section.

Upon hearing such an exchange, the stranger to our shores can't help but feel bewildered.

"What means this *fuck*?" he or she is likely to say.

The purpose of this book is to tell the newcomer just what this *fuck* does mean.

And what *shit*, *piss*, *cunt,* and *asshole* mean— along with a host of other terms that should be part of the vocabulary of any person who wishes to communicate effectively in the English tongue.

Our proven method is simple and to the point: We won't deal with complex grammatical matters— such as irregular verbs. When someone tells you: "I butt-fucked a goat," it should be obvious that such an action is irregular. Just ignore it.

There are books that will teach you to *avoid* using swear words.

They'll even teach you to avoid innocent words that might be *considered* swear words. Their point is to keep you from being thought of as vulgar.

We say, fuck it!

Vulgarity is not the point.

The name of the game is communication.

In the course of this work, we quote a number of poets. That shouldn't deter you. These are all *no-nonsense poets*. (There is one exception, and he is clearly identified.)

Because we're a panel of experts, we know what we're doing, and why we're doing it. We swear for one reason, and one reason only: It's the best fucking way to communicate!

Four centuries ago, Shakespeare—one of the greatest communicators the English language has ever known—put his stamp of approval on swearing. In *The Tempest* he has a character say:

> *You taught me language; and my profit on't*
> *Is, I know how to curse.*

The Bard had more to say on the subject. In *Henry V*, he shows us Katherine, a young French woman, as she takes a lesson in English. When she learns that the English words "foot" and "gown" sound like the French words *foutre* and *con*— "fuck" and "cunt"—she's delighted. She repeats them again and again.

Is this Katherine some kind of low life?

Far from it!

She ends up as Queen of England *and* France!

If swearing is good enough for Shakespeare and for the Queen of England *and* France— you can bet your ass it's good enough for us.

And for you.

The Basic Seven

In the 1970s comedian George Carlin cited the seven words you can never say on network T.V: These rank high in the building blocks of effective swearing.

- **shit**
- **fuck**
- **piss**
- **cunt**
- **asshole**
- **mother-fucker**
- **cock-sucker**

All these terms are now heard regularly on cable television. And for those who can read lips, they can be *seen* on all sports broadcasts. By the year 2001 they'll be heard on the more than 500 channels available to us—just one more example of how the Information Superhighway will enrich our lives.

Note of Interest 1:   Unlike such swear words as prick, screw, snatch, bung-hole, etc., these seven words can't be mistaken for anything other than swears.

Note of Interest 2:   Six of these terms can be used as "fighting words"—insulting words designed to provoke someone.

If you call someone a shit, a fuck, a cunt, an asshole, a mother-fucker, or a cock-sucker, you risk retaliation.

But call someone a "piss" and you'll only get a condescending smile.

Your intended victim will realize you haven't read *English as a Second F*cking Language*.

FUCK

Fuck is the mother of all words. Short and effective, it gets to the root of creation.

The euphemisms for fuck are cumbersome and inexact. One example will make our point:

example:

   Romeo: I want to **engage in sexual intercourse** with you.

   Juliet: Sorry, I don't have time. I thought you just wanted to **fuck**.

Some Romeo! What a namby-pamby mouthful! In the time it takes to say it, you could **fuck** a half-dozen times.

Fuck is sometime called **the F-Word**. Avoid that term. Just say **fuck.**

fuck

The word's meaning, both as noun and verb, is sexual and positive. However, many of its extended, nonsexual meanings can be negative.

example:

   Sigmund: How come you're mad at Carl?

   Rudolph: The no-good fuck fucked me out of ten dollars.

fuck around

    This sometimes means to fuck people other than your mate. It can also mean to engage in idle fun.

example:

    Dwight: Phoebe, dear, were you fucking around with anyone while I was at the shoe-clerk convention?

    Phoebe: Gosh no, honey. I spent my time fucking around by myself in the garden.

    Dwight: Odd. I found a used condom under our bed, and it wasn't mine.

    Phoebe: Huh, where do you suppose it came from?

fuck it

    The non-sexual meaning is similar to "the hell with it." It's a useful term for dismissing non-essential or irrelevant matters.

example:

    Nadine: Arnold, if we don't pay this phone bill by noon today, they'll shut off our service.

    Arnold: Fuck it. There's no one I want to talk to, anyway.

fuck up

    As a noun, **fuck-up** refers to a botched situation or an incompetent person. As a verb, **fuck up** refers to the action that caused it.

11

example:
> *Henry*:   That job turned out to be a real fuck-up.
>
> *Eugene*:   That's because that fuck-up Jackson was in charge. He could fuck up a wet dream.

Fuck you!

This is one of the most useful phrases in the lexicon of swears. It eliminates the need to argue—or even reason—with people whose purposes or opinions are different from your own.

example:

(**NOTE**: Marcel's words are italicized to indicate that he is acting them out rather than speaking them.)

> *Marcel*:   *Could you spare $5 to support the mime foundation?*
>
> *Frank*:   Fuck you!

example:

> *Officer*:   I'm sorry I had to ticket you, but the radar clocked you at five miles over the limit. Have a nice day!
>
> *Mort*:   Fuck you!

EQUIVALENTS OF FUCK

There are a number of equivalents for the word **fuck**. Our panel sees no need for them, but we offer a few for informational purposes.

VERBS

ball

This comes from the expression "to have a ball"—a good time. The "ball" in this case refers to a gala event, not a testicle. However, in order to ball, you need to have the testicular type of ball. You only need one, but two is the norm.

example:

Norm:	What happened with the girl you met at the ball last night?
Al:	She grabbed my left ball, so we left the ball and I balled her.

bang

Of the many aggressive words for fuck, this is the most common. Others include **boff** and **thump**.

examples:

Dexter:	Did I tell you I banged that blonde waitress from the Reno Diner?
Baxter:	I thought you said you boffed the redhead.
Dexter:	Right. I thumped them both
Baxter:	You sure have a way with the ladies!

dick

This term comes from the tool used in the act.

example:
> *William*: When does a gigolo bill his client?
> *Richard*: After he dicks her.

get it, etc.

Combinations with **get** that mean **fuck** include: **get a little, get in, get it, get it on, get laid, get some**, and **get your ashes hauled.**

hide the weenie

This is a jocular way to say **fuck**. Avoid it.

lay

This is a mild term for **fuck**, and a common one. It's based on the strange idea that people always lay down to fuck (see **basket fuck** in the IDIOMS section).

screw

Except in a **basket fuck** (see the IDIOMS section) there is no actual rotation involved. Like **fuck**, **screw** can have a negative, non-sexual meaning.

example:
> *Sergio*: I screwed up my math test; now I can't go on the class beach picnic.
> *Andre*: Then you won't get fucked; it looks like you're screwed.

NOUNS
lay
fuck
piece of ass
quickie

✳ ✳ ✳ ✳ ✳ ✳ ✳ ✳ ✳ ✳ ✳

FUCK ANALYSIS

Night at the Opera

John: Mary, would you like to attend the opera this evening?

Mary: Fucking-A[1]. Should I wear my black dress?

John: Why the fuck[2] not?

Mary: Fucked[3] if I know— Oh, fuck[4]! I just remembered. It got fucked up[5] in the wash.

John: Well, fuck[6] the opera, let's stay home and fuck[7].

Mary: Good fucking[8] idea.

1. **Fucking-A**: This is a strong affirmation.
2. **the fuck**: This is an intensifier.
3. **Fucked**: This is short for "I'll be fucked if I know," which has nothing to do with actual fucking. It's the equivalent of "I'll be damned if I know," which has nothing to do with damnation. In other words: "I don't know."

15

4. **Oh, fuck!** This is an interjection. The **Oh** isn't necessary; **Fuck!** by itself is a complete interjection.

5. **fucked up**: This means damaged.

6. **fuck**: Here, **fuck** is used in a negative sense, similar to, "The hell with the opera."

7. **fuck**: Here, **fuck** is used in its primary sense.

8. **fucking**: A novice might think the intended meaning is: "This is a good idea about fucking." In fact fucking in the sexual sense isn't intended; the word is merely an intensifier. And a fucking good one at that.

SODOMY

Said a jolly old chap from Siam:
"For fucking I don't give a damn.
You may think it odd o' me,
But I prefer sodomy;
They call me a bugger—I am."

Oscar Wilde

The jolly old chap in the poem had a preference for sodomy. For others it is merely a make-do arrangement, a substitute for fucking. Because of the dangers associated with the practice, our panel avoids it. One such danger was cited by Samuel Taylor Coleridge in *The Return of the Ancient Mariner*. In that epic sequel, the poet describes what happened when a reluctant cabin boy was subjected to sodomy:

. . . then that naughty little nipper,
He lined his ass
With broken glass
And circumcised the skipper.

'Nuff said?

17

NEED TO KNOW
ass-fuck
bugger
butt-fuck

NICE TO KNOW
bum-fuck
corn-hole
back-scuttle
Greek

FORGET IT
rear entry
back-door banditry

WARNING

LATIN TERMS

There is no need to give non-English names to our body parts. Avoid them. Such words often cloud rather than clarify the issue.

For example, the Latin word *vagina* is sometimes used instead of **cunt**. This is unfortunate. *Vagina* is easily confused with **Virginia**— particularly when abbreviated.

On the eastern seaboard of America, "the Commonwealth of Va." is a state; on the West Coast it's a two-block area of Sunset Boulevard.

The two parts that suffer most from this confusion are the *uvula* and *sternum*. Neither are sexual organs, yet the unwary often treat them as such. The results can be both unpleasant and dangerous.

There *are* exceptions. For certain sexual acts—such as *coginus* and *fensturbation*—there are no English equivalents. They should be used only in the original Latin, usually in whispers.

example:

    Camille: Doctor Benway, is *coginus* painful?

    Benway: Yes, if it's done right.

example:

    Wilma: What's your pet peeve, Bruce?

    Bruce: I hate those Liberals who are always saying *fensturbation* is normal and natural—until you do it in front of them!

HIS

The ancient Romans referred to the male organ as a *penis*. When in Rome, our panel does what the Romans do.

But we're not in Rome!

We call it a **cock**, a **prick**, or a **dick**—and a good many other names besides—but never a *penis*.

A number of names for the cock are common men's names. Besides calling a prick a dick, you might also call it a **peter**, a **willy**, or a **John Thomas**.

That may seem a little silly, but it makes more sense than calling it a **betty**, a **mary**, or a **lillian**.

The naming of dicks can go to extremes of delicacy. Sometimes the organ is not even mentioned.

examples:

Mary:	I just saw an old X-rated film with John Holmes. That guy was really big.
Bruce:	I suppose he *was* pretty tall—for an actor
Mary:	No—I mean he was really *big*.
Bruce:	Oh, yes. He was *very* successful— for a porn star.
Mary:	No—you needle-dicked moron! I mean he was really *BIG*!

21

This refusal to name the male member played a part in an excellent exchange of graffiti that our panel of experts traced to the "No Name" bar on Hudson Street in New York City. There, in 1965, an anonymous immortal wrote on the men's room wall:

"I'm 9 inches— are you interested?"

Beneath that, another immortal responded:

"Interested? I'm fascinated! But how big is your prick?"

Reluctance to mention the dick has a parallel in a common expression in which the dick is mentioned, but is absent; i.e., **dickless**. Logic tells us that the expression refers to women. Logic is wrong. It refers to men who show little courage or gumption. It's often used in combination with "wonder."

example:

    Stanley: How come Larry didn't make our men's group's annual whorehouse tour?

    Oliver: His wife wouldn't let him.

    Stanley: Jesus! That dickless wonder wouldn't stand up to a meter maid.

A dick exists in two states. The first is the limp state. In its proper place, there's nothing wrong with a limp dick— although when you call someone a **limp dick**, you're suggesting they're ineffectual— impotent.

example:

    Vernon: Gosh, I've got to pee really bad. I wonder if anybody would mind if I left the poker game for a few minutes.

    Rocco: No, you limp dick. In fact, we wouldn't mind if you left permanently.

Like Vernon, a limp dick can be pretty useless. On the other hand, you can't beat it when it comes to pissing.

However, when you *do* want to beat it, or fuck with it, or hang horseshoes on it—it had better be hard. Which brings us to:

HARD TIMES

A sage once observed, "A stiff prick has no conscience."

Other sages have confirmed that opinion. A man with a stiff prick is thinking of one thing—or variations of that one thing. The thing, of course, is fucking—or variations thereof.

The most common term for a stiff dick is a **hard-on**. It should be obvious how it got its name.

Other names for a dick in that state include:

blue-veiner:

So hard that blue veins are standing out on it in bas-relief.

example:

> Clem: How did your date with Suzie go?
>
> Jody: Not so good. Every time I looked at her I got such a blue-veiner it drained the blood from my head and I fainted. I never did get laid.

boner:

Seems to have a bone in it. This word can cause confusion, since "boner" also refers to a mistake or faux pas.

example:

> Annie: They tell me Chris committed a real boner by showing up at the nudist-colony dinner with a hard-on.
>
> Ginnie: I was there. *What* a boner!

diamond-cutter:

Hard enough to cut diamonds with.

example:

> Anita: A diamond is a girl's best friend.
>
> Marilyn: And a diamond-cutter ain't exactly her enemy!

rail:

   Also **rail on**. Both refer to a prick that's straight as a rail. The poet Kareem Roka described such a hard-on in the following verse:

   There once was fellow named Waylon,

   Who stood up in a boat with a rail on.

   "It's a mast," he declared,

   As his organ he bared,

   "And it's perfect for hanging a sail on."

rod:

   Also **rod on**. Both refer to a prick that's hard as an iron rod.

example:

   Nelson: My girlfriend is a hobosexual.
   Harold: Do you mean *homo*sexual?
   Nelson: No, *hobo*sexual. She likes to ride my rod.

stiffy:

   We won't patronize you by explaining this term.

BALLS

   "Balls!" cried the queen—"If I had them I'd be king!"

   from **Rudyard Kipling's**
   Queen Victoria's Lament

The word *testicles* is Latin for "little witnesses." Any man who wants to use that term to refer to his balls should be castrated. Don't get fancy: call them your **balls** or your **nuts**.

cod

This is a fine old word for the scrotum—the pouch that holds a man's balls. In the plural, it's used for the balls themselves. The word is most familiar in the expression **cod piece**, the decorative cup Elizabethan dandies wore to enhance their pants. Today, rock 'n' roll stars beef up their meat with cod pieces—in addition to such trouser-stuffers as potatoes, zucchinis, and rolled-up winter socks.

family jewels

Balls are as treasured as jewels and are definitely a family matter. Without them there would be no families.

nuts

This term is almost as common as "balls." The term "nuts" also describes someone who is crazy. Don't confuse the two.

example:

   Hector: Sigmund is crazy. He stood there on the podium in front of the TV cameras scratching his nuts.

   Andre: His nuts?

   Hector: His *nuts*!

   Andre: He's nuts!

nads

We're dead set against using a scientific term such as *gonads*, but we find this shortened form an agreeable substitute, if used sparingly.

example:

Placido: My, Luciano, your voice certainly seemed high during *Don Giovanni* last night.

Luciano: Yours would be too, if you'd been kicked in the nads by a 260-pound soprano!

rocks

Usually used in the expression **get one's rocks off**, meaning, to have an orgasm—to "come." **Rocks** can also mean "courage."

example:

Artie: Sam was screwing Louie's girl when Louie walked into the bedroom with a straight razor in his hand. Sam didn't pay any attention; he just kept going until he got his rocks off.

Jerome: Boy, Sam's sure got rocks!

Artie: Not any more he doesn't.

sack

The pouch that holds a man's balls. Sometimes called **nut sack**.

27

NEED TO KNOW

balls
cock
dick
hard-on
nuts
prick

NICE TO KNOW
cod
johnson
love Luger
one-eyed monster
pecker
peter
putz
rod
schlong
schmuck
skin flute
trouser trout

FORGET IT
banana
pee-pee tail
penis
wiener
weenie

HERS

Pardon, Madam, but I must be blunt—
I have to say I much admire your cunt.

Edward de Vere (1550-1604)

De Vere was a gentleman of the old school. True, he spoke bluntly— but always to the point. He could have called it "Love's sweet quiver," "the delta of Venus," "the tufted love mound"— or some other sort of poetic nonsense. But why pussy-foot around?

To quote the words of Robert Burns— another no-nonsense poet:

A cunt's a cunt for a' that.

cunt

The word "cunt" is specific—a wonder of clarity. The Latin term *vagina* is flawed. (See WARNING section.) Cunt is an old word, a solid word, a good word. Use it.

beaver

Because a woman's pubic hair seems like beaver fur to some people (although not to any member of *our* panel!), we call the visible area of the cunt a **beaver**. (See **shooting beaver** in the IDIOMS section.)

29

box

So named because it's a container for a prick. (See **box lunch at the Y** in the IDIOMS section.)

bush

Unless they're bald, all cunts are bushes.

coozy

Perhaps this comes from the word "cozy." Often shortened to **cooze**.

crack

Well, it looks like a crack—to the untrained eye.

down there

This odd phrase is used by parochial school girls, who learn it from the nuns. Don't confuse it with Australia, which is called "down under."

example:

Eve:　　G'day, mate. Would you like to touch me down there?

Adam:　　In Australia?

Eve:　　Not in the *continent*, you silly wanker! In the *cunt*!

hair pie

It looks like a *wedge* of pie rather than the whole pie. But there's no need to quibble—just enjoy a piece.

30

muff

If you've ever slipped your hand into the warmth of a cozy fur muff, you'll know where this term came from. If you haven't done that, just take our word for it: **Muff** is a good synonym for **cunt**. Used almost exclusively in combination with **dive**. (See **muff-diving** in the MATTERS OF TASTE section)

nooky

This can be used to describe an individual cunt. Usually it's used in the collective sense.

example:

Jan: You getting much nooky lately?
Dean: No.

pink

This collective term derives from the pink interior of a cunt. It came into vogue after popular magazines grew more explicit in their full-color spreads.

example:

Bradley: Have you seen the wonderful new Ansel Adams exhibit at the National Gallery?
Jeffrey: No. I lost interest in black and white photography after *Vogue* magazine started showing pink

poontang

The words **cunt**, **pussy**, **snatch**, **twat**, and **quim** are used in both the singular and the collective sense. **Poontang** is used *only* in the collective sense.

example:

Marie: You look so pensive Louis, standing there in the twilight, surveying the gardens below. What are you thinking about?

Louis: Poontang.

pussy

Furry, soft, and warm—but it doesn't go, "Meow." At least no one on our panel has ever known one that did.

quim

A nice old-fashioned word. Like **twat**, its origins are vague. Also, like **twat**, its prime meaning is **cunt**.

snatch

So called because pricks seem to be snatched into its confines.

Texas snapping turtle

A highly developed snatch.

example:
> Cody: Dang, Festus, your sister has got
>   herself a mighty talented snatch.
>
> Festus   *Snatch*? Hell, she's got herself a
>   regular Texas snapping turtle!

twat
See **quim**.

example:
> Stewardess: Would you like some of our TWA
>   coffee?
>
> Passenger: No thanks, but I'd love some of
>   your TWA tea.

vagina
Technical, Latin word for **cunt**. Avoid.

vertical smile
A bit poetic for day-to-day use, but a pleasant
concept anyway.

NEED TO KNOW
cunt
muff
pussy
snatch
twat

NICE TO KNOW
beaver
box

bush
cooze
coozy
crack
hair pie
pink
poontang
quim
Texas snapping turtle
vertical smile
whisker biscuit
wool, the

FORGET IT
down there
pee-hole
vagina

TITS

> *Stop where the truck drivers stop, and you'll*
> *always find a waitress with big tits.*
> **American folk wisdom**

The singular form is tit, but tits are usually discussed in pairs. The tit is made up of two parts:
　　1) the nipple;
　　2) the rest of the tit.

tits

The parts of a person's body with nipples on the end. Any reasonable discussion of tits concerns women's tits. Men have tits, but they're about as useful as a pair of extra appendixes.

balloons

This expression is based on the resemblance between tits and balloons. It is somewhat poetic. Avoid.

bazongas

These are *big* tits— bigger than **jugs** or **knockers**.

example:

Rocky:	Look at the bazongas on that dame!
Ernie:	Va-va-voom! She's a walking dairy!

boob

This alternative to **tit** is common, but can lead to confusion, since "boob" is also a term for a dopey person.

example:

Ben:	Look at the boobs on those dopey women!
Daniel:	Yeah, those boobs sure have nice tits!

hooters

This term is best reserved for describing owls.

jugs
    Big tits.

knockers
    Similar to jugs.

nipple leather
    This term is used mostly in discussions of tit sightings.

example:
    Lydia: How do you like my wedding gown?
    Sean: Too conservative. It doesn't show any nipple leather.

pair
    When the attributes of a woman are being discussed, **pair** is understood to mean "pair of tits," not "pair of feet," etc. (See **set**.)

set
    Because we're talking about **tits**, a **set** means a **pair**. Like pair, it can stand alone.

example:
    Skip: Maureen sure has a nice pair.
    Buzz: Yeah, a nice set.

NEED TO KNOW
boob
tit
pair
set

NICE TO KNOW
bazongas
jugs
knockers
nipple leather

FORGET IT
balloons
hooters
lungs
mammary glands
titties

EVERYBODY'S

"Opinions are like assholes; everybody's got one."

American folk wisdom

ASS

There are only two acceptable terms for this part of the body:

- **ass**
- **butt**

Of the two, **ass** is preferable.

The **ass** is that area you sit on. It consists of two parts:

1. the **cheeks**;
2. the **asshole**.

cheeks

The **cheeks** make up the bulk of the ass. They're sometimes called **buns**, or **chips**.

example:

Chuck: Hey, check out Betty's buns!
Pete: Sweet cheeks!
Chuck: Choice chips!

asshole

The **asshole** is dead center in the middle of the ass. When photographed from a distance it looks like an asterisk (*). As useful as the ass is, it gets little respect. It's frequently the basis for insults and putdowns.

ass eyes

A term of contempt. Our panel voted this our favorite putdown, primarily because it presents such stunning imagery.

example:

Stella: If you ask me, Stanley, you spend too much time watching professional wrestling on TV.

Stanley: Nobody asked you anything, ass eyes.

asshole

This term of disdain is best used to describe an arrogant self-centered jerk.

example:

Conrad: I wear my Mensa pin so people won't think I'm just some dumb asshole.

Vickie: Right. They'll realize you're some *smart* asshole.

ass kisser

A person who curries favor.

example:

Brendan: When I heard the boss was in the hospital, I rushed out to get him a dozen red roses, but all they had left was a bouquet of daisies.

Marge: It's the thought that counts, Brendan—you scheming little ass kisser.

ass-wipe

A cross between an asshole and a dip shit.

example:

Derek: Hey, how come everyone's leaving the theater?

Clark: Because the movie's over, ass-wipe.

kiss my ass

Similar to "Up your ass," but more personal. Often takes the form: "You can kiss my ass!"

example:

Steve: Can you give me the names of any babes in the Niagara Falls area who know how to show a guy a good time?

Marty: Kiss my ass, Steve. It's *my* sister you're marrying today, remember?

pain in the ass

This refers to an annoying person or thing.

example:

Harold: Bruno's acting like a pain in the ass today.

Maude: I think his hemorrhoids are acting up.

Harold: That explains it. They can be a real pain in the ass.

up your ass

The short form of "Stick it up your ass!" Sometimes shortened to "Up yours!" The expression is used to express disapproval or disagreement.

example:

Melvin: Belva, I seem to be a bit short of cash today. Would you mind picking up the check?

Belva: Up your ass, Melvin. You tried that stunt last week.

NEED TO KNOW

ass
ass eyes
asshole
ass kisser
buns
cheeks
kiss my ass
up your ass

NICE TO KNOW
butt
butt hole
chips

FORGET IT
bottom
derriere
heinie
rear end
posterior

TIPS AND TRAPS

Getting the words wrong

Type A: "Bastard to you, you
              big hell!"

Statements like the above will peg
you as a novice swearer. Bad
improvising is worse than no
swearing at all. Use the expressions
given in this book until you feel
completely at ease with swearing—
then you can show originality
without sounding like an asshole.

Type B: "This gosh darn mother-
              fucker isn't working
              right."

Much damage is done by trying to
soften your message by mixing
gentle euphemisms with solid
swearing. If you're going to swear,
go for it with both barrels.

Subtleties

Mark Twain's wife once tried to cure him of swearing. To show him how awful his swearing sounded, she let fly with a lengthy string of curse words.

When she finished, Twain commented: "The words are there, my dear, but the music is wanting."

Good point.

To swear effectively, you must pay attention to tone.

For instance, it's wrong to say:

Why don't you go fuck yourself?

Forget the question mark. Say:

Why don't you go fuck yourself!

You're not asking a question—you're *exclaiming*! It's a matter of tone.

Originality is not essential to effective swearing. Nor is a wide vocabulary necessary. However, as you develop your skills, you'll learn subtleties.

Novice: "Hey, **asshole**, get out of here."

Master: "Hey, **ass eyes**, get out of here."

To show scorn for someone by calling him an **asshole** is perfectly acceptable. It delivers the message that you hold the person in low esteem.

But how much more elegant to call him **ass eyes**. You deliver the same message, but with an enhancement— you paint a vivid picture.

Jokes.

If you tell jokes in English they had better be dirty. Dirty jokes in English are much funnier than non-dirty jokes. This is easily shown:

Clean Joke:

Q. Why did the chicken cross the road?
A. To get to the other side.

Dirty Joke

> *Wally*: Hey, honey, what do you say to a little fuck?
> *Beth*: Hi— you little fuck!

See?

BY THE NUMBERS

Pissing and shitting are sometimes known as the numbered body functions. They're, respectively, #1 and #2. Our panel assumes that's merely an alphabetical ordering, since the two functions are of equal importance.

Some experts think they're numbered so that people won't have to name the objectionable material that is ejected from the body, namely: piss and shit.

Our panel doesn't accept that theory. We don't number the processes that void our snot, puke, or ear wax. Why should we give preference to piss and shit?

PISS

Some people will tell you that piss gets its name from the sound it makes. That's ridiculous. Pissing is the silent function. The only sound pissing makes is when the piss strikes something.

If piss strikes water, it makes a gurgly sound, but we don't say we're going to "take a gurgly."

If piss strikes a cymbal, it makes a tingly sound— as anyone who's ever attended a Grateful Dead concert can tell you— but we don't say we're going to "take a tingly."

Why it's called piss is beside the point.

piss

As a verb it means to empty your bladder. It can be used alone or in the form "take a piss."

example:
> *Vern*: I'm going to take a piss.
> *Eugene:* Me too. I've got to piss so bad my teeth are floating.

piss

As a noun, it is the water that you empty from your bladder.

example:
> *Bob*: I've been thinking of saving my piss in gallon jugs.
> *Ted*: Why?
> *Bob*: I dunno. Just an idea.

As noun and verb—and in combination with other words—piss has a number of meanings.

piss off

To anger; to upset.

example:
> *Luther*: You piss me off, Marvin.
> *Marvin*: How come?
> *Luther*: Because you keep pissing off my balcony into my geraniums.

piss off

As a command it means "Get out of here!" "Get lost!"

example:

"Piss off! Can't you see I'm busy?"

pissed

Similar to "pissed off"

example:

"I was really pissed when they repossessed my car." (*Note*: you can say, "They pissed me off," but not, "They pissed me.")

pissed

Intoxicated

example:

"I was so pissed from drinking home brew I couldn't walk."

piss away

To waste, as time or money.

examples:

Herman pissed away his inheritance on slow horses and fast women.

Adele and Louise pissed away the afternoon talking about Herman.

piss

As a noun, piss can be used to signify an inferior beer or other liquid.

48

example:
>   *Kurt*:   Care for a nice glass of lite beer?
>   *Virgil*: No thanks. I can't drink that piss.
>   I'll have a Jack Daniels on the
>   rocks.

NEED TO KNOW
piss
pee

NICE TO KNOW
bleed the lizard
drain the dragon
drain the monster
take a whiz

FORGET IT
do #1
go see a man about a dog.
tinkle
wee-wee
make water

SHIT

This is a good straightforward word. To shit is to
empty your bowels. Everybody does it, and
everybody knows what it means. So why do so
many people try to skirt the issue?

If there's any problem at all with the word, it's with the past tense. It's the question our panel of experts is most often asked. Here's a typical letter of inquiry from a reader.

> *Q*: Dear Panel: Should I say "I *shit* yesterday," "I *shat* yesterday," or "I *shitted* yesterday?"
>
> *A*: Dear Reader: If you really wish to discuss past bowel movements with others, you may say either "I shit yesterday," or "I shat yesterday."

shit
> As a verb it means "to empty one's bowels." As a noun (see below) it refers to what was emptied from those bowels, namely: shit.

example:
> *Reader*: I shit yesterday.
> *Panel*: You said that already. Quite frankly, we don't care when you shat, or if you ever shit again!

Shit may also be used as a transitive verb; that is, you may say what it is that you're shitting. However, only do so if what you're shitting is something unusual.

example:
> "I shit a brick." (See the IDIOMS section.)
> "I shit a porcupine." (See a good proctologist.)

50

Under most circumstances it is enough to say simply: "I shit."

Note: Under no circumstances should you say "I shit a shit." It is redundant, and makes you sound like an ignorant shit.

shit

As a noun, *shit* really comes into its own. Like the word "stuff," it can stand for almost anything. Surprisingly, it has positive as well as negative connotations.

example:

Elgin:	That new venereal disease going around is really bad shit.
Roy:	That's why I always carry a jar of penicillin with me—it's really good shit.

bullshit

As a noun, bullshit means nonsense or fakery. As a verb, it means to try to trick someone through using bullshit. As a stand-alone term, it is a rebuttal to such bullshitting.

example:

Jason:	I'll have that money for your first thing tomorrow, and that's no bullshit.
Fred:	Bullshit! That's what you said yesterday. Don't try to bullshit an old bullshitter.

dip shit

A stupid person, or one lacking in awareness.

example:

Lenny: Gee, Nancy sure acted cold to me at the supermarket.

Fred: Not surprising, dip shit. You were supposed to marry her last Saturday but you left her standing at the altar.

Lenny: Oh, yeah. I forgot.

cheap shit

This refers to worthless advice or other unwanted commentary.

example:

Margo: Purvis, don't you think it's about time you shaved, showered, and changed those socks?

Purvis: Margo, when I want a ration of cheap shit from you, I'll squeeze your head. Now step out of the way—this is an important game I'm watching.

tough shit

A difficult state of affairs. It is sometimes used in the abbreviated form: **T.S.** It is usually used in cynical responses.

example:
> Allen: We've got to read all of T.S. Eliot's poetry for our mid-term exam.
>
> Lionel: Tough shit. You only have to *read* it. He had to *write* it—the poor bastard.

shit-head

This refers to a person. Such a person's head is not actually stuffed with shit, but it might as well be. A shit-head is a worthless person, a mean-spirited person, a person you don't want to spend any time with.

example:
> Velma: My brother Earl talked those orphans into signing their inheritance over to him.
>
> Arnold: Your brother Earl is a shit-head.

NEED TO KNOW
shit
crap
take a shit
take a crap

FARTS

Q: *Why do farts smell?*
A: *So deaf people can enjoy them too*.

This gets to the heart of the fart. It's a two-fold phenomenon. Note, however, there's only one word for it: **fart**.

Some people call the emitting of gas from the bowels "flatulence." Stick with "fart." Noun or verb, you can't beat it. Attempts to do so will only cause trouble and confusion.

For instance, a common term for the act of farting is "breaking wind."

A "windbreaker," though, is not a person who farts, but a type of clothing.

Imagine the confusion that might ensue if, say, a new clerk in an upscale clothing store like Barneys New York was not familiar with the stock.

Customer: I'd like a windbreaker, please. Something tasteful, you know—nothing too loud.

Clerk: You have obviously come to the wrong place. I suggest you try Barney's Beanery in Los Angeles.

End result: The store loses a customer and—if the boss is around—the clerk loses a job.

Another term for farting is "passing gas." This term also creates confusion. Picture the scene:

Reggie and Yvonne are driving through the Louisiana bayous en route to a fun-packed weekend in New Orleans. They're running low on fuel. Reggie looks to his left at what appears to be a whooping crane or, possibly, a pair of mating alligators. Thus distracted, he speeds past an exit with a "Gas" sign. Yvonne panics.

Yvonne: Reggie! You passed "Gas!"
Reggie: I did *not*! That's just swamp vapors.

You can see where that relationship is headed. So much for the fun-packed weekend in New Orleans!

Further examples are unnecessary. The word is **fart**, and a good word it is.

fart
As a verb it means to emit gas from the bowels; as a noun it is the emission itself.

cut a fart
To fart.

cut the cheese
To fart, especially to let rip an SBD.

let a fart
> To fart.

let one rip
> To fart.

old* fart
> An old fool, a fuddy-duddy; often a term of affection.

fart around
> To engage in leisurely, pointless activity; to goof off.

example:
> Teacher: Albert, the correct answer to today's problem is "six yards of silk at \$6.57 per yard." What in the heck is "$E=mc^2$" supposed to mean?
>
> Student: Please forgive me, Mein Herr, I vas just farting around.

SBD
> Silent but deadly: the type of fart that puts the hearing-challenged on an equal footing with everyone else.

LBH
> Loud but harmless: the type of fart that is only half as embarrassing as it could be.

The word "old" is often used to modify swear words; through its use, what might be considered an offensive term can become a good-natured term of affection.

example:

Angus:	I'm sick and tired of all these young people running around naked, taking drugs, and listening to rock and roll music.
Vivian:	Oh hush up, you old fart.

Or:

Gene:	Duke, you old son of a bitch, how do you feel today?
Duke:	Just fine, Gene, you old bastard, how 'bout yourself?

Warning! The one swear word you must not modify with "old" is "bitch." It will be considered neither an affectionate nor a good-natured term.

example:

Nephew:	Aunt Sarah, you old bitch, how do you feel today?
Aunt:	Since you ask, Jason, I feel like disinheriting a certain nephew of mine. And how do *you* feel today, you vulgar little cocksucker?

BLASPHEMY

Blasphemy is definitely not what it used to be—certainly not in the English-speaking world. Gone are the days when such curses as "God's Wounds!" (often shortened to "Zounds!") raised an eyebrow.

In other parts of the world you can have your head cut off for blaspheming. Or worse— your balls! That's one reason our panel avoids other parts of the world.

If you want to blaspheme, do it in English, and keep it simple. Stick with the following terms. They're all you need.

damn
Usually a stand-alone filler, as in "Damn! that's good chicken."

damn you
See **goddamn you**.

damn *or* **damned**:
An intensifier. "That's damn good chicken."

goddam, goddamn
  or **goddamned**
Used in the same senses as damn. "That's *goddamned* good chicken!"

goddamn it

An expletive, usually used to express displeasure: "Goddamn it! Leave my chicken alone!"

goddamn you

This is an odd construction. Literally, it's a way a person prays to his or her God to condemn someone to spend eternity in Hell (see below). Although that sounds fairly severe, it's generally considered a mild rebuke nowadays.

example:

"Goddamn you, Wilbur, stop picking your nose in church."

Hell

This is the place where bad people are supposed to go after they die. Its climate varies from religion to religion. In some it's fiery; in others, it's icy. There are usually devils and demons around to make things even worse. Hell is unpleasant and long lasting, but just what bad people (our enemies) deserve.

hell

A mild filler expression of annoyance or exasperation.

example:

"Ah, hell, Leroy, stop pestering your sister."

It's used with "in" or "the" to intensify question words.

examples:

"What in hell are you cooking, Emma?"
"Where the hell are my socks?"
"Why in hell does this soup taste so funny?"
"Who the hell put my socks in the kettle?"

It's also used with "of a" to indicate something is either good or bad. The meaning depends on the context.

examples:

Dad: Putting socks in the soup was a hell of an idea, Tommy.

Tommy: (smiling) A hell of a good one, Dad?

Dad: (swatting Tommy) A hell of a bad one.

Jesus, Christ, Jesus Christ, Jesus Christ Almighty

Usually a stand-alone filler, as in: "Jesus Christ Almighty! Will you stop talking about that goddamn chicken!"

FAMILY MATTERS

Who's that coming down the track,
Prick and balls slung o'er his back?
Well, strike me dead!
It's Foreskin Ned—
The Bastard from the Bush!

Australian folk ballad

Technically speaking, a **bastard** is the child of unwed parents and a **son of a bitch** has a dog for a mom.

But we're not speaking technically—we're communicating.

Today, there is no longer a stigma behind being the child of unwed parents. In some rural areas of the United States there's not even that much stigma behind having an animal for a parent.

The two terms have taken on a life of their own.

bastard
When you call someone a **bastard**, you're leaving their parents out of it. You're implying the person is a generally mean-spirited or despicable person.

example:

> *James*: That bastard Jones fired me for sticking my dick in the potato peeler.
>
> *Rick*: The potato peeler?
>
> *James:* Yeah, Bridget, the redhead. And the son of a bitch fired her too.

son of a bitch

As with **bastard**, parentage isn't the issue. A **son of a bitch** is just a mean-spirited and despicable person.

example:

> *Paddy*: That son of a bitch Jones fired my girlfriend, Bridget.
>
> *Seamus*: Did she get into something she wasn't supposed to?
>
> *Paddy*: Vice versa.

NOTE: The above terms apply to men only. A woman who exhibits the tendencies of a **son of a bitch** or a **bastard** is properly referred to as a **bitch**.

Son of a bitch is sometimes used to express surprise or delight. It's meaning is close to that of the Greek term "Eureka!"

example:

> *Socrates*: I think you'll like this. It's a mix of gin and vermouth with an olive dropped in for decoration.
>
> *Archimedes*: Son of a bitch! It's delicious. You've finally come up with a good idea.

HANDS-ON EXPERIENCE

Under the spreading chestnut tree
The village blacksmith sat
Amusing himself
By abusing himself
And coming off in his hat.
— **Henry Wadsworth Longfellow***

Most American lads learn this poem at about the same time they learn to masturbate. Masturbation is sometimes called self-abuse by those who claim not to do it. There are no official statistics on who *does* do it. Based on our own experiences, our panel estimates it's practiced by about 100% of the population.

It's not a newfangled concept. Mark Twain noted that masturbation was common to such great artists of the past as Michelangelo, Da Vinci, Rubens, and Rembrandt. The term "The Old Masters," he observed, was only a nickname.

---

* Supposedly Henry Wadsworth Longfellow was the real name of the poet who penned that verse. Our panel members are a bit leery about the middle and last names. If the poet's

The more common names for this singular pastime are:

beat the dummy

The hand movement tells the story. It seems a shame to refer to the dick as a dummy. After all, that's where most men's brains are located.

beat the meat

If you have to ask, you'll never know.

choke the chicken

Of mysterious origin. Our panel feels it has something to do with the expression, "A bird in the hand is worth two in the bush."

flog the dog

This is the only case our panel has ever heard of a dick being called a "dog." There's no reason for it, except that it rhymes with "flog." It makes about as much sense as saying, "festoon the balloon." If you *insist* on rhyming, something like "jostle the throstle" would make more sense. We recommend you stick with **jerking off**.

ham-boning:

When the hand grips the dick as snugly as the meat on a roast ham grips the ham bone, you have mastered the art of ham-boning.

---

first name had been Peter or Dick we'd be sure the name was a fraud. But none of us has ever heard anyone call his prick a Henry. We'll accept the poet's name as legitimate—for now.

example:

Luther: Doctor, I've sustained a repetitive-stress injury in my wrist from constantly ham-boning off. Can you help me?

Doctor: First, I'll help you with your grammar. Just say "ham-boning." The "off" isn't necessary. You wouldn't say "jerking off-off." Don't say "ham-boning off!"

Luther: Thank you doctor. And what about my wrist?

Doctor: That depends. Do you have medical insurance?

jerk off

The term comes from the jerking motion employed. To call someone a "jerk" is to suggest that he spends too much time jerking off. The poet Algernon Charles Swineburne described that type of situation movingly.

There once was a fellow named Merkin,
Who always was jerkin' his gherkin.
Said his girlfriend, "Hey, Merkin,
Stop jerkin' your gherkin,
Your gherkin's for ferkin' not jerkin'."

66

The expression is sometimes used to mean "patronize".

example:

    DeWitt: My boss jerked me off for a while, telling me what a good worker I'd been. Then he fired me.

    Clinton: What for?

    DeWitt: He caught me jerking off at my desk.

jack off

A variation on jerk off. School children delight in crying out: "Stop the bus and let my brother Jack off!"

know thyself

This expression was a favorite of Plato's. He uses the verb "to know" in the Biblical sense of "to have sexual intercourse with"—or, in English, "to fuck." Thus: "fuck thyself."

pound off

Based on the pounding motion used.

pound the pudding

The "pound" makes sense—but why the "pudding?" Some scholars say it comes from the Latin *pudendus*—"something to be ashamed of." Others feel it comes from the Scottish term for a sausage. Our panel favors the second theory. We don't feel anybody should be ashamed of his sausage.

practice self abuse

This is a silly term. There is nothing abusive about jerking off, and it requires no practice. When you "practice jerking off," you are, in fact, jerking off. However, it's a useful term, if only because it gives us an insight into the mind of Henry Wadsworth Longfellow.

pull off

Another term derived from the motion employed. It can cause confusion, as in the report of the eager bridegroom who, on the way to his wedding, "pulled off on the side of the road."

pull the pud

"Pud" is short for "pudding," but it's pronounced to rhyme with "mud."

peel the eel

A Canadian term, restricted to the Maritime Provinces and Vancouver Island.

stroke off

This term is self-explanatory. Men and boys sometimes stroke off while looking at pictures of naked women. Magazines that contain such pictures are called "stroke books," or—for obvious reasons—"one-handers."

whack off

Here again, the movement of the hand suggests the name.

COME

Among males, the end product of masturbation is *semen*—the vital male generative fluid. This marvel of nature is the source of all human existence, and is impossible to remove from suede.

"Semen," like most scientific terms is misleading, particularly when spoken. For example:

A **merchant seaman** hangs out on freighters.

A **semen merchant** hangs *it* out at sperm banks. Avoid confusion: Stick with the following terms.

The Noun:

come

Derived from "coming off." Sometimes written as **cum**.

example:

Elvis: Dang! What the heck's that on my footwear?

Parker: Looks like cum spots to me, son. I warned you to lay off of them blue suede shoes.

jism

There are a number of variant spellings. Among them are: **gizm**, **jizzum**, and **jissom**. There's also the shortened form: **giz** or **jizz**. No one knows the origin of the word. One of our panelists notes that it rhymes with "prism." The rest of say, "So what?"

wad

The amount of cum emitted in an orgasmic transaction. Usually used in the expression **shoot one's wad**.

example:

Fifi: Hey, Marvin, why are you stopping?

Marvin: I've shot my wad. It's time to get home to the wife and family.

duck butter

No one on our panel has ever heard this term used.

The Verb:

come

This is the most commonly used term for achieving orgasm. It's the short form of **come off**. To avoid confusion, it's often written as "cum." Unfortunately, when spoken, it's often confused with other senses of the word "come."

examples:

Q. What's gray and comes in quarts?

A. An elephant.

Or:

Mother: You've been in that bathroom for half an hour, Lewis. We're all packed and ready to leave. Are you coming or not?

Lewis: Not yet, Mom—but I'm breathing hard!

cream
   Usually used in the expression **cream one's jeans**—which is the process of "coming off in one's pants." (See Pound poem below.)

get off
   The same as **come off**. Sometimes elaborated as **get your nuts off** or **get your rocks off**.

shoot a wad
   See **wad** above.

Orgasms are produced by various means, most of which involve friction of some sort. Some, however, are spontaneous—gifts from the cods, so to speak. Here again, we must turn to poetry to get a full understanding of such phenomena. Although unsigned, the following is believed to be one of Ezra Pound's early outpourings.

> *There once was a lady from France*
> *Who got on a train in a trance.*
> *Everyone fucked her,*
> *Except the conductor,*
> *And he came off in his pants.*

MATTERS OF TASTE

Q: *How does a Frenchwoman hold her liquor?*
A: *By the ears.*

No one knows when that riddle first appeared in print. However, several of the cunning linguists on our panel of experts recognize that it has long been a staple of the oral tradition in English-speaking lands.

The French are generally considered (by English-speaking people) to be the masters and mistresses of oral sex. That mastery, along with their knowledge of *savate*—kick-boxing—is the stuff of legends. Those skills have been immortalized in the following poem.

> *The French they are a funny race;*
> *They fight with their feet and fuck with*
> *their face.*

The English term "Frenching" has historically been applied to *any* act of oral sex. Have the French truly earned their high ranking in this area? It's not as certain as a mathematic proof, so we can't swear by it. But we must note that it is the French who have given the world the term *soixante-neuf*—69.

Because of the position of the 6 and 9 relative to each other, *soixante-neuf* has become the international mathematical symbol for mutual oral sex. This has led to yet another riddle:

Q: *What's the square root of 69?*
A: *Eight something.*

Here again, the riddle is more accessible within the oral tradition than the written.

But enough of such reflection. It's time to get to the meat of the matter.

COCK-SUCKING

You call a guy a cock-sucker, that's an insult.
You call a lady a cock-sucker—
hey, that's a nice lady.

Lenny Bruce 1926 -1966

The technical term for this activity is *fellatio*, and a sillier term would be hard to imagine. Rely on **cock-sucking**, a term that everyone can readily understand.

73

blow

> This is a common—but slightly misleading—term. It has caused more than one gentleman to beseech his lady, "Don't blow—suck!"

NEED TO KNOW
blow
eat
give a blow job
give head
go down on
French
suck
suck off

NICE TO KNOW
give a B. J
gobble the goose
lick dick
polish the helmet
suck dick
take a lip lock on a fuck stick

FORGET IT
eat a weenie
lick the lollipop

MUFF-DIVING

> *The proof that God isn't a woman is that*
> *men's dicks aren't on their chins.*
> **Sappho** (*circa* 600 BC)

Being an ancient Greek, Sappho didn't use the English term **muff-diving** to describe her favorite pastime—licking a lady's lower lips. But unless you're an ancient Greek, *you* should.

We've listed a selection of equivalents, but **muff-diving** is the most widely used and understood.

NEED TO KNOW
eat
eat out
eat cunt
eat pussy
French
go down on
muff dive

NICE TO KNOW
eat a box lunch at the Y
eat hair pie
eat the bearded clam
go lickety split
munch a fur burger
suck cunt
suck pussy

FORGET IT
slurp the slit
cannibalize the cunt

IDIOMS

It's hard to say where a lot of idioms come from. Some you can figure out, but many seem to defy all logic.

Don't let that bother you. Just learn them and use them.

basket fuck
A technique for fucking involving a bottomless basket suspended by a rope-and-pulley arrangement. The woman sits in the basket and lowers herself onto the dick of the man below. As the fuck commences, she pulls on the rope, raising it and lowering it at an ever-increasing tempo. He spins the basket.

example:
> *Lawrence*: That Mabel is the dizziest blonde I've ever seen.
> *Antoine*: A result of too much basket fucking.

built like a brick shithouse
This term is used to describe a shapely woman. It might be used to describe a shapely man, although none of the experts on our panel has ever heard it used that way.

A shithouse is the term for an outhouse, a small structure, usually wooden, where people can shit and piss. Why anyone would think a shapely woman looked like an outhouse is a mystery. The fact that it's made of brick deepens the mystery.

example:

    Lenny: Look at that shapely woman.

    Vince: Yeah. She's built like a brick shithouse.

coming air

This term describes the orgasmic state of a man who is "fucked out." He has come so many times he has exhausted his supply of jism. That kind of overload sometimes results in death. Undertakers hate such cases, since it can take hours to remove the smile from the dead man's face.

example:

    George: Alonzo, you look plum worn out. Didn't you get any sleep last night?

    Alonzo: Hell no. Janet and I had an all-night fuck fest. By the time the sun came up I was coming air.

Eat shit!

The ideal expression when "just saying no" is not enough.

example:

Wally: Hope I didn't wake you. I'm doing an insurance-needs assessment and I wonder if you'd mind answering a few questions about your family's current security umbrella.

Jack: Eat shit!

the fuck

This fragment does not refer to a particular act of fucking. In fact, it's about as far from a fuck as you're likely to get—unless, of course, you're a celibate.

It's a handy little interjection to beef up a sentence.

example:

Ralph: What the fuck did you do to my bowling ball?

Wilbur: You think I tampered with your bowling ball, Ralph? The fuck I did!

Ralph: Ah, get the fuck out of here!

No one knows why the fuck "the fuck" is used. Suffice it to say, it's a useful term.

fucking the dog

> *Old Mother Hubbard*
> *Went to the cupboard*
> *To get her poor dog a bone.*
> *When she bent over*
> *Rover took over,*
> *For he had a bone of his own.*
>
> **Percy Bysshe Shelley**

The idiom **fucking the dog** would *not* apply to the above poem. Furthermore, Shelley—unlike the other poets cited in this book—was definitely *not* a no-nonsense poet. Our panel of experts wanted the poem included here purely on aesthetic grounds.

In point of fact, there is no lusty canine involved in "fucking the dog." The expression refers to more or less random behavior that borders on idleness.

example:

Judge: You've been out on the street six months now, Lamar, and you still haven't found a job. What the hell have you been doing with your time?

Lamar: Oh, not much—just fucking the dog, I guess.

lip lock on a fuck stick

This melodious phrase is a fancy way of describing a blow job. Poetic, but acceptable.

liver box

A feature of Army life, the **liver box** is a shoe box with a hole cut in one end. The box is filled with warm liver and covered. Then it's fucked.

mother-fucker

This sounds like the bottom-line description of someone with an Oedipus complex. In fact, it might describe anything from an evil villain to a lima bean. (G.I.'s in Vietnam referred to their ham-and-lima-bean C-rations as "ham and mother-fuckers.") Once a terrible curse word, it now ranks with "thingamabob" and "whatchamacallit."

example:

Billy: Mr. Rogers, give me three of those red jelly beans and four of those green mother-fuckers, please.

Rogers: My, Billy, you're a polite little mother-fucker.

Billy: That's 'cause Mom is strict as a mother-fucker about politeness.

nooner

This is the classic lunch-hour fuck. It is often a **quickie**, although with proper planning it can be extended to a full sixty minutes, give or take a few seconds for fly zipping and unzipping and skirt hoisting and lowering. Although it traditionally takes place between noon and 1 PM, in enlightened workplaces it is a staple of morning and afternoon coffee breaks.

example:

    Josie: How has working the graveyard shift affected your love life?

    Sam: Not much, except now I get my nooners at 4 in the morning.

piece of ass

This is not a butt chunk. One sense of this term is **a fuck**.

example:

    Mavis: Why so sad, Roy? You look like you need a hug.

    Roy: Hug? What I need is a good piece of ass.

The expression can also be used to describe a person who is especially good at fucking. Curiously, it can also describe someone who is just an average, run-of-the-mill fucker.

example:

    Arlo: That was a swell-looking gal I saw you with last night. She looked like a real piece of ass!

    Lamont: Nah. She was just some piece of ass I picked up at the diner.

quickie

Love on the run. This is the classic fast fuck. It is *intentionally* fast. A fuck that's fast because the guy shot his wad too soon is not a **quickie**. It's just a lousy fuck.

R.C.H.

These initials stand for **Red Cunt Hair**. The term originated with the master carpenters of Cape Cod, and is now universally used. An **R.C.H.** is considered to be the smallest non-microscopic measurement known to man.

example:

Asa: Hondo, this board don't fit just right. Looks to me like it ain't got enough littleness.

Hondo: Well, don't force it, you goddamned moron! Just take an R.C.H. off the end.

shit a brick

This means to react strongly when surprised or startled. It can be used in either a positive or a negative sense.

example:

Alice: When my mom won the lottery, my dad damn near shit a brick.

Bernie: Yeah, and when she took off to Hawaii with the Sears delivery man he damn near shit another one.

shit happens

This fatalistic statement is often seen on bumper stickers. In this idiom, shit refers to events and circumstances beyond our control. Usually it refers to those conditions of life we don't welcome, but which we must learn to live with.

example:

John: After the pit bull bit me I headed for the hospital on my motorcycle, but I got hit by a bus and knocked into a briar patch. That's when the hornets nest fell on me.

Mary: Shit happens.

shooting beaver

This is the practice of looking up women's dresses in the hope they're not wearing panties. Baseball players lucky enough to be outfielders spend much of their times scanning the stands for such views.

example:

Rip: Boy! what a great game I had today.

Ty: Great game!? You struck out four times, made three errors, and allowed the winning run to score from first base on a routine pop fly.

Rip: Yeah, but I shot seven beavers, two of them natural blondes!

Stop jerking me off

This sound like an odd request. If you allowed someone to *start* jerking you off, why in the world would you want them to *stop*? The fact is, the "jerking off" in this expression means using flattery to curry favor.

example:

    Clyde: Gee, Mr. Fenton, that's one of the smoothest golf swings I've seen since the company golf tournament started.

    Fenton: Stop jerking me off, Clyde! Not only did I miss the ball, but the club slipped out of my hand and flew about fifty fucking yards.

    Clyde: That's true, Mr. Fenton, but it landed right in the middle of the fairway in great position.

    Fenton: A point well taken, Clyde. By the way, you're fired.

you bet your ass

This term is a resounding affirmative. It's about as upbeat and positive as anything in the arsenal of swears. Who would suggest betting such an essential body part as this unless they were sure of the results?

example:

    Mary: Do you think we ought to fuck?

    John: You bet your ass I do.

The Final
F*cking Exam

It's time to test your swearing skills.

Circle the letter next to the *best* answer to each of the following questions. You have fifteen minutes to complete the exam. If you need more time, take it.

BEGIN:

1. Your boss passes you over for a promotion that he promised you. You're angry and decide to quit on the spot. He begs you to stay until you've wrapped up an important project. He says you're the only one in the company who can finish it.
You tell him:
a. "No way—you've bastarded me long enough!"
b. "Tough pussy! I'm leaving now."
c. "Fuck you!"

2. A shapely young woman walks by a construction site while the workers are taking their lunch break. She is wearing a tight red miniskirt. Her hips sway hypnotically as she passes. One man eyes her intently, then turns to a co-worker and says:

    a. "Wow! Look at the sternum on that babe!"

    b. "Gee! That gal is built like a brick cocksucker!"

    c. "Nice ass."

3. You're dining at a five-star restaurant and have ordered the house specialty, Roast Squab with Almond and Truffle Stuffing. Twenty-five minutes after taking your order, your waiter returns to your table. He tells you that the kitchen has run out of squab and asks if you'd like to order something else. You get to your feet and say:

    a. "What a big fart this turned out to be!"

    b. "This place is a cunt."

    c. "Fuck it—I'm grabbing a burger at McDonald's."

4. A tornado destroys your neighbor's home. While he is surveying the damage, he's mugged by a passing felon. When he awakens he discovers his wallet, his car keys, and his car are missing.

    After he tells you of his woes, you say:

    a. "You must feel like a real prick."

    b. "You poor bitch."

    c. "Shit happens."

5. You buy five lottery tickets at a dollar apiece. You hit on one of them, winning $3.6 million. The other four don't pay off. You don't complain, though. You shrug your shoulders and say philosophically:

    a. "What a pain in the uvula."

    b. "Well, at least one of them jerked off the dog."

    c. "What the fuck—you can't win 'em all."

6. John and a lady friend spend a wild weekend of sex. On Monday a co-worker comments on John's bedraggled appearance. He describes his recent activities, adding:

    a. "We fucked so much I was finally climbing into the air."

    b. "We fucked so much I finally combed my hair."

    c. "We fucked so much I was finally coming air."

7. After drinking four bottles of beer in fifteen minutes, Arthur heads for the bathroom to:

    a. peel his eyes

    b. skin his cat

    c. bleed his lizard

8. Jim is having a 4th of July party at his house. About 2 A.M., a neighbor shows up at his door and complains about the loud music and noisy fireworks. He is smaller than Jim, and Jim notices that he isn't armed.

Jim says to him:

    a. "Talk to me in stilted fucking lingo."

    b. "Take a fucking lug-wrench to your flag staff."

    c. "Take a flying lip-lock on my fuck stick.

9. You're told that a certain woman can "suck the chrome off a trailer hitch." That should suggest to you that:

    a. she is good hearted

    b. she gives her heart away

    c. she gives good head

10. Mary goes out on a blind date with a Texan who's supposedly a big spender. She expects him to show her a spectacular night on the town. Instead, he takes her to a shabby cowboy bar and spends the evening trying to sell her a time-share in a Horizon City condominium.

    She later describes him as:

    a. a fucking realist with a lasso

    b. a fucking Realtor from El Paso

    c. a real fucking asshole

Scoring is as follows:

    10 points for every *c*. answer

     0 points for every *a*. answer;

     0 points for every *b*. answer;

You must score 100 points to pass the exam. If you don't pass the exam, take it again. Continue taking it until you do pass.

Remember—if a fucking thing's worth doing, it's worth doing fucking well.